Especially
for the
Hurting Heart

Especially for the Hurting Heart

by
Robert Strand

New Leaf Press

First printing: April 1997

Copyright © 1997 by New Leaf Press. All rights reserved. Printed in the United States of America. No part of this book may be used or reproduced in any manner whatsoever without written permission of the publisher except in the case of brief quotations in articles and reviews. For information write: New Leaf Press, Inc., P.O. Box 726, Green Forest, AR 72638.

ISBN: 0-89221-348-5
Library of Congress Number: 97-65170

Cover by Steve Diggs & Friends, Nashville, TN.

All Scripture references are from the New International Version, unless otherwise noted.

Presented to:

_____

Presented by:

_____

Date:

_____

1
When Life Comes Crashing In

The classic, beautifully restored MG moved briskly through the busy afternoon traffic. The driver enjoyed the quick response of the small high-powered English-built convertible. After driving her eight-passenger van, this little red car was rather like taking off heavy work clothes and putting on a jogging suit. Driving along with the wind in her hair, she tried to look casual and at ease with herself and the world around . . . but inside, she was a bit tense since she didn't often drive this car . . . her husband's pride and joy.

She saw only a blur of color out of the corner of her eye. Before she could consciously consider her actions, she swerved to miss a small boy on a bicycle and veered into the side of a large gray 4 x 4 pickup truck! The little car stopped with a deafening "ker-thunk-crash!" For a second there was the tinkle of falling glass and the splash, splash, splash of antifreeze from the radiator . . . then all was quiet for what seemed like a long time.

"Hey, lady! You okay?" Strong arms reached and lifted her from the vehicle and helped her to the curb, where she sat.

"I'm fine, I think," she said. "Just let me sit here for a little bit."

All she could think of was, *I'm fine now, but Jim's going to kill me when I get home.* As she waited for the police to arrive, she recalled how excited he was when he found this car. He had wanted one ever since he was a boy. This one was a rare treasure and he had spent countless Saturdays restoring it, fixing it, cleaning it, and polishing it. He knew every bolt and spot of chrome. It wasn't really his wrath she feared . . . he was actually a gentle and loving husband. But she dreaded the hurt and anguish she would see in his face when he heard the news. That, for her, would be far worse than if he were to get angry and yell. *Thank God, I'm not hurt,* she thought, *but I sure am worried about telling Jim.*

Her head was bent down and she saw the highly polished boots stop at her feet, "May I see your driver's license and insurance papers, miss?" The officer felt sorry for her. He thought, *What a great little car that was.*

She walked to the car, got her purse, and grabbed the insurance package from the glove compartment. She gave the officer her license and opened the plastic package that contained the insurance papers. To her surprise, there on top of all the documents was a white envelope with her name on it.

She opened it and began to read: "Dear Beth, If you are reading this, you have probably been in an accident. Don't worry. I pray that you are all right, and just remember it's YOU that I love, not the car. Jim."

The cross of Calvary is God's statement for all who hurt for all time: REGARDLESS OF HOW YOU MAY HAVE WRECKED YOUR LIFE, REMEMBER, IT'S YOU THAT I LOVE!

For all of us . . . when we hurt, when we have had a life-wreck, when we are struggling with disease, when we are depressed, when we are looking for answers, when life has crashed in around us, when we have sinned, when we have messed up . . . one of the hardest things to deal with is this sense of hurting God, disappointing God. His message to you today is simply this: YOU ARE THE MOST IMPORTANT THING IN ALL THE WORLD TO ME! Believe it! Don't let anybody or anything rob you of the comfort of His love in your life when it's needed most!

Today's Quote: "Adversity is the diamond dust Heaven polishes its jewels with." (Robert Leighton)

TODAY'S BIBLE VERSE: "For I am the Lord, your God, who takes hold of your right hand and says to you, Do not fear; I will help you" (Isa. 41:13).

SUGGESTED BIBLE READING: Isaiah 41:1–29

The Bible's Most Encouraging Verse

Dr. Tim LaHaye claims to have asked more than 100,000 people across America this question: "Is there anybody here who has never been discouraged? Raise your hand." He goes on to say that no one, among the folks questioned, has ever raised a hand.

Depression and discouragement are both ancient and universal to the human race. It's here with us today. It's a constant battle. You can find it devastating people in all strata of lifestyles. What does the Bible have to say about it?

My nomination for the Bible's most encouraging verse is taken from Hebrews 13:5, "God has said, 'Never will I leave you; never will I forsake you!" This is solid gold from the Word and it does not stand alone. You can read this same promise from the Old Testament sources of Deuteronomy 31:6 and Joshua 1:5.

WHAT DOES "NEVER" MEAN? This is something special. We go back to the original language in which it was written to discover that it is really a compounding of five negatives. Not that each negative is added to another, each negative is multiplied by the other. It should really read, "I will never, no, not ever, no never leave you or forsake you"! It is a synergistic compounding negative. It's a forever never which has no exceptions!

WHAT DOES "LEAVE" MEAN? Again we refer to the Greek language to find that this word is *aniemi*. It's the second aorist active subjunctive, which in our language will translate something like this: "to leave behind, to abandon, to give up on, to send back." Well, then, so far our verse will read: "I will never, no not ever, no never leave you behind, abandon you, give up on you, or send you back!" Such words need to become a part of your internal thinking. If God doesn't leave you behind, He is taking you along!

WHAT DOES "FORSAKE" MEAN? Here is another fascinating word as found in the Bible. It's another of those Greek words, *encatalipo*, which translated means, "to leave one in a helpless state, to disregard." It also can be further expanded to include "not relaxing my watchfulness over you." To this point, then, our verse, in the full, amplified version reads: "I will never, no not ever, no never give up on you, abandon you, leave you behind, cause you not to survive, leave you helpless, nor shall I ever relax concerning keeping my presence with you!" Awesome!

The Rev. Jess Moody, pastor of a California church, relates:

Arthur Ray Ebersol had drowned. The paramedics were working over his body. The frantic father was begging the paramedics and the boy for a sign of life. I, as his pastor, had been called along with the medical emergency team. I took in this entire scene on a Southern California beach, as I arrived. I made my way to the circle of medics and people around Arthur.

As the drowned boy was being worked on, suddenly, in the background, we all heard a voice . . . clear as crystal, a female voice ringing with hope. All eyes turned in the direction of the song. It was Arthur's mother, sitting in the cab of the paramedics' truck. She was looking up through the open sunroof and affirming her faith skyward in song:

> No! Never alone. No! Never alone.
> He promised never to leave me,
> Never to leave me alone!

TODAY'S QUOTE: "As sure as God puts His children into the furnace of affliction, He will be with them in it!" (Charles H. Spurgeon)

TODAY'S BIBLE VERSE: God has said, "Never will I leave you; never will I forsake you." So we say with confidence, "The Lord is my helper; I will not be afraid. What can man do to me?" (Heb. 13:5-6).

TODAY'S SUGGESTED BIBLE READING: Hebrews 13:1–25

Nearer My God

The Reverend Charles Treptow, of Lufkin, Texas, writes: A face of grace and a handshake firm escorted me on my initial encounter with Bill's relaxed and pleasant presence. Bill was a mortician in a small Texas town. And as life surprises our beings, we found ourselves working together on many an occasion.

Bill had a means of making the journey from the church house to the cemetery an enjoyable and memorable experience.

He would sing and hum his favorite hymns as we discussed and drove, leading a procession of cars to the graveyard on the edge of town.

Wisdom can be gleaned from other folks if one respects and listens to the soul, and in looking back, I received many insights from Bill into the human condition at death and burial time.

Once Bill told me, "You never know what song is in the heart of a person. But if you listen to the words from their mouths, you can hear their melody."

One winter day we journeyed together to Brenham for an interment! On the way Bill shared his soul's secret stories and songs. His life was lived much like his lyrics. And he would sing a poem of passion as the car's motor kept time.

Pastors tend to move on and leave behind a portion of their souls and songs, memories and music, and Bill became a lost friend.

Years elapsed and a message emerged informing me that Bill had succumbed to a stroke. He was paralyzed and unable to speak. His hospital sojourn was lengthy and minimum recovery proved difficult.

After many weeks, Bill's wife was able to take him home. There she would care, cook, clean, and cater to Bill. He could not speak; Bill could hardly move. And so the silent saga lingered on.

Following many months of persistent silence, one morning his wife dressed Bill and placed him in the day room for his morning sunlight.

A brief period elapsed when she heard Bill singing. Singing. Singing!! After all those silent months. Now he was singing.

Bill caroled the entire hymn, "Jesus Loves Me," followed by "Amazing Grace." No verses were omitted. Each word was clear. Every syllable was articulated with precision and clarity of voice. Bill's wife called their close friend to "come over here right now. Bill is singing."

Their friend and neighbor came running over and heard Bill's distinct voice halfway through "What a Friend We Have In Jesus."

"Bill, can you hear me? Talk to me, Bill," intoned his wife and friend.

But Bill kept on singing, not missing a note. Omitting no verses. Not answering their questions. No talking! Only singing.

The last words he spoke and the final song he sung was "Nearer My God To Thee." No words were omitted. No verses were skipped.

Bill lies silent now, resting after a long and laborious path of faith and life.

"You never know what song is in the heart of a person. But if you listen, you can hear their melody."[1]

TODAY'S QUOTE: "Entrance into heaven is not at the hour of death, but at the moment of conversion." (Benjamin Whichcote)

TODAY'S BIBLE VERSE: "Not everyone who says to me, 'Lord, Lord, will enter the kingdom of heaven, but only he who does the will of my Father who is in heaven" (Matt. 7:21).

SUGGESTED BIBLE READING: Matthew 7:1–29

4
Six Operations . . .
and Finally, Victory!

It looked like life was about over for Ione Soltau, dean of women at North Central Bible College in Minneapolis, Minnesota. The doctor's diagnosis was that her cancer was terminal.

The struggle began in 1959. She says, "Little did I realize as I closed my office door that August 30, that the Lord was ushering me into a very different box of my life."

Three times in the next few weeks she found herself quoting Psalm 23 ("The Lord is my shepherd . . .). Then each time before six surgeries she repeated that Psalm to herself.

Prayer sustained Ione, and each time her recovery surprised her two doctors, who were fine Christians and gave credit to God.

One of them told Ione before her fifth operation, "What our God has done before, He can do again."

Then in 1963, Ione was admitted to the hospital once more and underwent a sixth operation. This time the doctors told her they could do no more for her. The cancer could not be surgically removed. The verdict was metastasis, cancer in the bloodstream.

Friends surrounded Ione with prayer. More than 45 pastors and their wives visited and prayed for her. Her church, the college, and friends across the country held prayer meetings to pray for her. Some at times prayed around the clock.

God answered prayer, though the healing came slowly. She continued as dean of women at the college for years; she has been a teacher of art and has had her own showings. She has been a popular speaker at summer camps, children's crusades, and churches. The healing was indeed a new beginning for her.

Thirty years later, in 1993, Ione Soltau was still free of cancer and still active. Every time one of her doctors sees her, he says, "You are my miracle. I must believe in a God of miracles."

Ione says, "Every added day of living is an adventure in serving the Lord."[2]

Yes . . . God can heal and does heal. "Divine" healing can be instantaneous or take place over time, slowly. He is a source and power over and above what medical science can do. But we are also aware that healing may come through the divinely inspired techniques and skills of a trained medical doctor. Healing is a mystery. Why are some people healed and some who seem so worthy are not healed, physically? I wish I could give you a definitive answer as to the reason why.

Upon reading the biblical account we discover that at least on one occasion, Jesus Christ himself could do no mighty miracles,

"And He was amazed at their lack of faith" (Mark 6:6). Contrast that to just a little bit of time previously and we read, "The whole town gathered at the door, and Jesus healed many who had various diseases" (Mark 1:33–34).

How do you account for the difference? Here, it apparently was a lack of faith on the part of the people. Yet we can read in many other places that others were healed because of the faith of somebody else, and not of the person being prayed for. An example is when Jesus was teaching in a house and there was a clamoring outside because there was no way to get to Jesus, who was on the inside. So these men, carrying their paralyzed friend, raised the roof and lowered him down into the presence of Jesus. We read that "When Jesus saw their faith, He said to the paralytic, 'Son, your sins are forgiven . . . I tell you, get up, take your mat and go home' " (Mark 2:5, 11).

I can't explain it to you . . . but this one thing I know, "Everything is possible for him who believes" (Mark 9:23).

If you need a physical or spiritual or mental healing . . . KEEP ON BELIEVING, KEEP ON PRAYING, and ASK OTHERS TO PRAY AND BELIEVE WITH YOU! God can do it again!

TODAY'S QUOTE: "God heals, and the doctor takes the fee." (Benjamin Franklin)

TODAY'S BIBLE VERSE: People were overwhelmed with amazement. "He has done everything well," they said. "He even makes the deaf hear and the mute speak" (Mark 7:37).

SUGGESTED BIBLE READING: Mark 7:1–37

5
Brian's Song

When Gale Sayers and Brian Piccolo, both running backs for the Chicago Bears, began rooming together, it was a first for race relations in professional football. It was also a first for both of them. Sayers had never had a close relationship with a white person before, with the possible exception of George Halas, and Piccolo had never really known an African-American person.

One secret of their growing friendship lay in their similar tastes in humor. Before an exhibition game in Washington, for instance, an earnest young reporter entered their hotel room for an interview.

"How do you two get along?" the writer asked.

"We're okay as long as he doesn't use the bathroom," said Piccolo.

"What do you fellows talk about?" asked the business-like reporter, ignoring the guffaws.

"Mostly race relations," said Gale.

"Nothing but the normal racist stuff," Piccolo added.

"If you had your choice," the writer went on, "who would you want as your roommate?"

Sayers replied, "If you are asking me what white Italian fullback from Wake Forest, I'd have to say Pick."

But submerged beneath the horse laughs and the digs lay a fierce loyalty to each other, and as the moving movie *Brian's Song* poignantly depicted, the friendship between Sayers and Piccolo deepened into one of the best relationships in the history of sports. Then during the 1969 season, Piccolo was cut down with cancer. He fought to play the season out, but he was in the hospital more than he was in the games. Gale Sayers flew to be beside him as often as possible.

They had planned, with their wives, to sit together at the Professional Football Writers annual dinner in New York, where Sayers was to be given the "George S. Halas Award" as the most courageous player in pro football. But instead Pick was confined to his bed at home. As he stood to receive the award, tears sprang to Sayer's eyes. The ordinarily laconic black athlete had this to say as he took the trophy: "You flatter me by giving me this award, but I tell you here and now that I accept it for Brian Piccolo. Brian Piccolo is the man of courage who should receive the George S. Halas Award. I love Brian Piccolo and I'd like you to love him. Tonight, when you hit your knees, please ask God to love him, too."

"I love Brian Piccolo." How often do we hear men say words such as these? But how much more enriched our lives could be if we dared to declare our affection as did Sayers that night in New York.[3]

Brian Piccolo died soon after, losing his battle with cancer. But think a bit with me about how his life had been enriched by a friendship, a relationship that withstood the ravages of a crippling, death-dealing disease. We all need a close friend, but especially so when we are grappling with things that hurt and cut, devastate and kill.

The Bible says this about such a friendship: "Two are better than one, because they have a good return for their work: If one falls down, his friend can help him up. But pity the man who falls and has no one to help him up!" (Eccles. 4:9–10)

TODAY'S QUOTE: "We can never replace a friend. When a man is fortunate enough to have several, he finds that all are different. No one has a double in friendship." (Schiller)

TODAY'S BIBLE VERSE: "Though one may be overpowered, two can defend themselves" (Eccles. 3:1).

SUGGESTED BIBLE READING: 1 Samuel 20:1–42

6
The Risk of Reaching . . .

It was an afternoon in the early summer; there was a strange quiet on the battlefield. In the bright sunshine, the air was balmy and had a breath of garden in it. By some grotesque miracle, a bird was singing somewhere near at hand.

On the firing step, with his rifle lying in a groove in the parapet, stood a private soldier in field-gray, his uniform stained with mud and blood. On his face, so young yet strangely marked with the lines of war that made him look old, was a wistful, faraway expression. He was enjoying the sunshine and the quiet of this strange lull in the firing. The heavy guns had been silent . . . there was no sound to break the eerie stillness.

Suddenly a butterfly fluttered into view and alighted on the ground almost at the end of his rifle. It was a strange visitor to the battleground . . . so out of place . . . so out of keeping with the grim setting, rifles and bayonets, barbed wire and parapets, shell holes and twisted bodies. But there it was . . . a gorgeous creature, the wings like gold leaf splashed with carmine, swaying in the warm breath of spring.

As the war-weary youngster watched the butterfly, he was no longer a private in field-gray. He was a boy once more, fresh and clean, swinging through a field in sunny Saxony, knee-deep in clover, buttercups, and daisies. That strange visitor to the front-line trenches recalled to him the joys of his boyhood, when he had collected butterflies. It spoke to him of days of peace. It was a symbol of the lovelier things of life. It was the emblem of the eternal, a reminder that there was still beauty and peace in the world . . . that somewhere there was color and fragility and perfume and flowers and gardens.

He forgot the enemy a few hundred yards across no man's land. He forgot the danger and privation and suffering. He forgot everything as he watched that butterfly. With all the hunger in his heart, with the resurrection of dreams and visions that he thought were gone, he reached out his hand toward that butterfly. His fingers moved slowly, cautiously, lest he frighten away this visitor to the battlefield.

In showing one kind of caution, he forgot another. The butterfly was just beyond his reach . . . so he stretched, forgetting that watchful eyes were waiting for a target. He brought himself out slowly . . . with infinite care and patience . . . until now he had just a little distance to go. He could almost touch the wings that were so lovely.

And then . . . ping . . . ping! A sniper's bullet found its mark. The stretching fingers relaxed. The hand dropped flat on the ground. For the private soldier in field-gray, the war was over. An official bulletin issued that afternoon said "all is quiet on the Western front." And for a boy in field-gray it was a quiet that no guns would ever break.

There is always a risk . . . when you reach for the beautiful. When you reach out for the lovelier, finer, more fragrant things of life . . . there is always a risk . . . and you can't escape it.

The risk is what makes the Christian life so exciting. It is thrilling . . . make no mistake about it. It is an adventure.

As long as we live in this world, there will always be a risk in reach![4]

TODAY'S QUOTE: "It is only by risking our persons from one hour to another that we live at all. And often our faith beforehand in an uncertified result is the only thing that makes the result come true." (William James)

TODAY'S VERSE: "You have been raised with Christ, set your hearts on things above, where Christ is seated at the right hand of God" (Col. 3:1).

SUGGESTED BIBLE READING: Colossians 3:1–17

7

The Power of a Human Touch

It's still a vivid memory for me, and to think I almost blew it!

While pastoring a church in Grand Junction, Colorado, I also served as a member of the Community Hospital Board of Directors. This was in the era of time when AIDS was first being identified and the medical community was attempting to come to grips with this issue. As a board, we struggled with what we were to do and how we were to handle our first AIDS patients. Little was known about the disease other than that it might be highly contagious.

Out of discussions with medical specialists, a hospital policy was tooled out. Among other things, isolation was prescribed, which meant that anyone entering this room had to be gowned up, masked, and gloved before administering any kind of treatment or care.

Well, it wasn't long after that when the first person with AIDS was admitted to the hospital. Isolation it was. The patient was a young man, now in the last, final, advanced stages of the disease. A pitiful young man whom no one came to visit. The only people he had any kind of human exchange with were medical people behind their protections. It was a lonely time, a time when family and friends should have been there for him. But he had been abandoned to die alone in the hospital.

Because of his loneliness, and the lack of understanding of the disease, the isolation was unbearable. The hospital people were unable to get any clergy to stop to help him . . . so one day I received a call from the hospital administrator, "Pastor, would you be so kind as to make a visit with our first AIDS patient? We can't get anybody else, because of fear. Because you are a member of our board and understand some of the problems, we feel that you're the likely one."

"Thanks . . . a whole lot. Okay, I'll make a visit," I answered with more bravado than I felt.

Upon preparing for entering the room, the isolation nurse helped me to cover up. First there were throwaway booties over my shoes, then a gown that covered me from shoulders to feet, followed by a mask, goggles, and finally gloves. Then she cautioned, "Don't touch the patient or anything in the room and when you come out, discard all of these things and then scrub up vigorously." I gulped. . . .

I entered the room and through the mask introduced myself to a curious young man. We made polite conversation. Then got serious . . . we talked about the things of God and preparing for the imminent death he was facing. We moved to the point where it was time to pray . . . nothing seemed to get through to him to this point.

I prayed silently, "God help me, what should I do?"

Then, I felt prompted to remove my goggles, which I did, then the mask, which I did, and my gloves, which I did. I reached for his hand . . . and he began to cry as I held his hand in mine. He said, "Since I have been in the hospital with AIDS, no one has touched me. . . ." And he sobbed. "You are the first real human touch without a glove."

Then we prayed together, he in his tears, me in my tears. I felt condemnation — I had treated him like an untouchable, something to be abhorred, something less than human. I asked the Lord to forgive me.

And yes . . . I was able to lead him in praying a sinner's prayer. I followed up that visit with only two more before he passed on into eternity. Oh, I must tell, you, when I came out of that room rejoicing, I was met by the charge nurse who said, "You did what?!"

As I drove away, there was both condemnation and rejoicing. What if I had not touched him? Would he have accepted the Saviour I professed to serve if I had been unwilling to touch him?

TODAY'S QUOTE: "Security is mostly a superstition. It does not exist in nature, nor do the children of men as a whole experience it. Avoiding danger is no safer in the long run than outright exposure. Life is either a daring adventure or nothing." (Helen Keller)

TODAY'S BIBLE VERSE: Filled with compassion, Jesus reached out His hand and touched the man. "I am willing," He said. "Be clean!" Immediately the leprosy left him and he was cured" (Mark 1:41–42).

SUGGESTED BIBLE READING: Mark 1:14–45

8

A New Pattern of Thinking

Ralph Waldo Emerson said, "A man is what he thinks about all day long."

I propose that the 23rd Psalm is really a pattern of thinking, and when a person's mind becomes saturated with it a new way of thinking and a new lifestyle can be the result. It contains only 118 words in the familiar King James translation. Most of us know it already . . . but its power is not in memorizing the words, but in thinking the thoughts, living the message.

The power of this short Psalm lies in the fact that it represents a positive, hopeful, faith-filled approach to life. It was written by David, who had a black chapter or two in his life, but found the answer to living life as it should be lived, looking forward, trusting in the shepherd.

THE LORD IS MY SHEPHERD. . . . This Psalm doesn't begin with asking God for something, rather it's a calm statement of fact.

Before we needed heat, God began storing up oil, coal, sunshine, and natural gas to keep us warm. He knew we would be hungry, so before He put mankind on this earth, God put fertility in the soil, rain in the skies, and life in the seeds.

One of the greatest sources of human worry is about tomorrow and God has simply told us not to worry because the plans have already been made and carried out.

Because the Lord is our Shepherd . . . all kinds of blessings begin to flow as you would continue on reading through the Psalm. He leads, He restores, He is with us, He takes away our fears, He comforts, He protects, He is always planning ahead, He heals, and He promises!

One of the most exciting benefits is the assurance that we can dwell in His house forever.

John Howard Payne had been away from his home for nine years. One afternoon he stood at a window watching the throngs of people, happy, hurrying, going home. Suddenly he felt lonely, there in his Paris hotel. He turned from the window, he had work to do, but the mood and memories wouldn't leave him. He picked up a pencil and wrote:

> 'Mid pleasures and palaces though we may roam,
> Be it ever so humble, there's no place like home.

David brought this beautiful expression of praise to a mighty crescendo of faith when he declared: "I will dwell in the house of the Lord forever!"

One of the those heart-stirring passages from Bunyan's *Pilgrim's Progress* is that in which "Mr. Feeble Mind" speaks of his hope of home. He says: "But this I am resolved on: to run when I can, to go when I cannot run, and to creep when I cannot go. . . . My mind is beyond the river that hath no bridge, though I am, as you see, but of feeble mind."

There is a story of an old man and a young man on the same platform before an audience. A special part of the program was being presented. Each of these men was to repeat from memory the 23rd Psalm. The young man, trained in speech and drama, gave in oratory, the Psalm. When finished the audience clapped for more so that they could hear his beautiful modulated voice once more.

Then the old man, leaning on his cane, stepped to the front of the platform and in a feeble, shaking voice, repeated the same words. But when he was seated no sound came from the listeners.

Folks wiped tears as they seemed to pray. In the ensuing silence, the young man again stepped forward and made the following statement: "Friends, I wish to make an explanation. You asked me to repeat the Psalm with your applause, but you remained silent when my friend was finished. The difference? I shall tell you. I know the Psalm, but he knows the Shepherd of the Psalm."

TODAY'S QUOTE: "Change your thoughts and you change your world." (Dr. Norman Vincent Peale)

TODAY'S BIBLE VERSE: "I was young and now I am old, yet I have never seen the righteous forsaken or their children begging bread" (Ps. 37:25).

SUGGESTED BIBLE READING: Psalm 23:1–6

Losers Can Become Winners Too!

Thomas Edison made 18,000 different experiments before he perfected the light bulb. Dr. Jonas Salk worked 16 hours a day for over three years to perfect the polio vaccine, failing many times in the process. Paul Ehrlich, a chemist, worked day and night for years to perfect a chemical simply called "606" which would destroy the germ that causes syphilis. Why 606? Because the 606th experiment was the success, thus the name!

One person said to me following a message about successful living, "Well, so much for the winners, but what can you do for a loser like me?" If you are hurting because of some failure or setback or struggle, hold on, let's take another look. I believe that losers can become winners, too!

Life is filled with stories of upsets when all the computer predictions and expert projections are thrown to the wind. Your life can become another inspiring upset story.

I know of a person who flunked the first and fourth grades and went on to become an astronaut . . . Ed Gibson.

I know of someone who ran for public office seven times and was defeated every time and still went on to become president . . . Abraham Lincoln.

I'm thinking of somebody who was kicked out of the psychiatric society in Vienna who went on to become one of the most prominent and respected psychiatrists . . . Dr. Viktor Frankl.

Michelangelo was confronted with a huge chunk of marble that had been cast aside by sculptor after sculptor because it was too long and too narrow. When asked what it was for, he said, "I see David in it." He chiseled and carved and polished and when he finished, sure enough, there was David standing tall.

Rise Stevens, one of the greatest sopranos of all times tells the story of how she went out for a competition hoping to win, because the first prize meant that she would be the soprano soloist of the air on a "National Radio Network." She prepared for years for this opportunity, she hired a great coach/instructor/teacher and borrowed thousands of dollars to pay for her lessons. She practiced and practiced until the coach was sure she was ready. Then she went into the competition. She made it to the semi-finals. Now the choice was between Rise Stevens and one other soprano. She performed and went back to her private dressing room to await the judging outcome.

Finally, the phone rang . . . it was the chief judge. He said, "Miss Stevens, I'm very sorry to tell you that you were not selected. I'm sorry because I thought your voice was the best, but the other judges felt the other person had more experience."

Rise Stevens continued, "He went on but I didn't hear any

more. I put down the phone and looked through my tears at my coach. I'd borrowed thousands of dollars to pay him. Now I had nothing. I'd be known as a loser.

"My coach looked at me and didn't say anything that I thought he should have said. He should have said, 'It was politics,' or 'She isn't nearly as good as you are.' But he didn't. He simply got out of his chair, walked over to me and said, 'Miss Stevens, all I can say is, have courage to face your faults. Your next lesson will be at 2:00 this afternoon.' "

And for two more years he hammered away at her faults. That was the beginning of greatness. Then there was the European tour and she came back from Europe heralded by America for a great career.

TODAY'S QUOTE: "Success is never certain and failure is never final."

TODAY'S BIBLE VERSE: "I can do everything through Him who gives me strength" (Phil. 4:13).

SUGGESTED BIBLE READING: Philippians 4:1–23

Miracles Can Happen in Your Life

Miracles can happen! And they can happen in your life! Wonderful things are possible for you! Astonishing events can become a part of your experience!

Why am I so sure of this possibility? Because over many years, I have seen it happen again and again! So I know it can happen to you!

Personally, I have an enormous respect for church and a church service. It's a time when people gather and subject themselves to the effect of an atmosphere that is vital, dynamic, and exciting! There is uplifting music, prayer and praise, and the preaching of God's Word, which can all light a spark that ignites a person.

In such an atmosphere personalities can change, burdens are lifted, sin is repented of, sicknesses can be healed, family life changed, and new life begins! Where does the source of such power come from? "To all who received Him, to those who believed in His name, He gave the power (right) to become children of God" (John 1:12).

That word "power" or "right" is from the original word, *exousia* meaning privilege, force, capacity, freedom, mastery, authority, right, and the strength. It's something we can't do in ourselves. Jesus Christ is the essence of it! Here's how it worked out in one family:

The first time I met "Smiling Jim" McCloskey, or better known in our area as "Cowboy Jim," a popular entertainer, I liked him. We were looking for a church custodian. He showed me his union entertainer's card and we talked.

It came out that Jim was an alcoholic, down to his last cent, looking for help. His wife had just told him, "No more, I'm leaving if things don't improve." His kids had agreed to leave him, also.

I noticed that Jim walked with a limp and he explained: "Pastor, that happened when I was drinking. I would get so drunk I'd pass out for three or four days at a time. It's cold in Wisconsin and as I lay out in my car, dead drunk, I froze my feet so bad they had to amputate my toes and part of my foot. But still, I kept on drinking."

Soon no one would hire him for a gig or work. He told me he hid bottles, he told how he could tell the time of the night by how much was left in his bottle at his bedside. He told of the rejection, frustration, guilt, and no help that helped. He'd been in and out of institutions and hospitals and programs, but just kept on getting worse.

Finally, he looked at me, "Pastor, I can't go on and I can't find a cure. Can you help me, do you think God can help me?"

We knelt right there for prayer, and we both prayed and cried.

As he left, we walked outside into a beautiful summer day, lawns were closely cropped and green, overhead was a blue sky into which Jim looked and cried, "Dear Jesus, I can't do it! I can't make it! I can't stand my life or myself any longer! Please, Lord Jesus, HELP ME!"

Later, Jim told me, "All of a sudden, at that moment, I felt strangely clean and happy and strong. From that moment, standing on the church steps, I mastered my problem!"

We hired Jim to be our custodian. He showed up for church and brought the whole family. On their first Sunday morning, Mrs. McCloskey and two beautiful kids walked down the aisle as Jim led them to also accept Jesus Christ.

I'll never forget the baptismal service which followed a couple of weeks later. His eleven-year-old son just sobbed as he said to the crowd, "Since Jesus came into my dad's life, I love him, and home is nice, now!" Jim wept as he expressed his gratitude for the miracle. Mrs. McCloskey wept as she talked of the change in Jim's life. The preacher wept and the crowd wept, as together we rejoiced in the miracle!

TODAY'S QUOTE: "Every believer is God's miracle." (Philip James Bailey)

TODAY'S BIBLE VERSE: "I am not ashamed of the gospel, because it is the power of God for the salvation of everyone who believes" (Rom. 1:16).

TODAY'S SUGGESTED BIBLE READING: John 1:1–34

11

Lilies from the Dirt

Lilies, in order to become white, do not need to grow in white sand. Instead, they often thrive in the some of the darkest, most putrid and dirty soils imaginable. They have even been known to grow in coal mines. The pure white blossom is a sharp contrast to the dirt from which it gets life. It's a paradox that this emblem of purity springs from the earth which is anything but pure and white.

The truth we have just applied to the lily can also be true of many of God's choicest people. The rarest blooms are often found in the most unexpected of places. Among the many salutations scattered through Paul's writings is one nugget that illuminates this truth about the gospel and the grace of God. Paul is hunched over in a Roman dungeon, writing a letter to the church at Philippi. Then, as an encouragement to those believers in that Macedonian city, he included special greetings from all the believers in Rome, "All the saints salute you," and adds, "chiefly they that are of Caesar's household" (Phil. 4:22)!

It's a surprise enough that there were Christians in Rome, but doubly so that some were in the very household of the emperor, who was such a hater of Christians. He had tortured and martyred all the believers he could lay his hands on and now there were saints right under his very nose, slaving in his palace!

This Caesar, who was ruling at the time Paul was writing this letter, was none other than the infamous Nero! History reveals that few, if any, were worse rulers than this scandalous despot. He has been described as "half-man and half-monster." His lifestyle was so horrible and depraved as to defy description. One of his crimes was the murdering of his own mother! He often illuminated his gardens by the light of burning Christians used for torches. For recreation, he'd go into the streets disguised for the purpose of murdering people for the fun of watching them die. He was a total scoundrel, a sensualist, a tyrant, selfish, self-centered, lustful, disgrace to humanity. His palace was a pigsty of moral filth.

Yet . . . in the midst of these surroundings and somewhere in the employ of this diabolical ruler, there were Christians radiating the glory of God! Likely they were among the vast hordes of slaves who ministered to the wants and whims of the wicked wretch Nero. Many would reason that no person could possibly live consistently the life of a believer under such circumstances. Yet, according to the Apostle, there were saints in this household.

There are some life-principles that jump out at us from this obscure little verse:

1. People living for God can be found in some of the most unlikely places.

2. Living a Christian life is not dependent upon locality.
3. God is able to overrule evil and make something good out of it.
4. It is possible to live for God under all kinds of tough situations, anywhere.

And, so, my hurting friend, take heart! God's grace is greater than environment or circumstances. The factors that turned these people into saints were internal rather than external. They were lily-white in spite of surroundings rather than because of them! You can live for God no matter what!

TODAY'S QUOTE: "I never met with a single instance of adversity which I have not in the end seen was for my good. I have never heard of a Christian on his deathbed complaining of his afflictions." (Alexander M. Proudfit)

TODAY'S BIBLE VERSE: "And we know that in all things God works for the good of those who love Him, who have been called according to His purpose" (Rom. 8:28).

SUGGESTED BIBLE READING: Romans 8:18–39

12

Little Billy Bob Robinson

The Rev. John Wilder tells the following story.

When I first knew them, the Sam Robinsons were operating a little two-story frame hotel near the border of Texas and Mexico. Mr. Robinson also worked with a road-grading machine for the county.

They were a large family of well-behaved children and were respected as humble Christian people. Mr. Sam was not a preacher, but I heard him preach a sermon one day that after more than 30 years still stands in my memory as one of the greatest I ever heard. And that sermon had only 13 words.

Most of the Robinson children were about grown when little Billy Bob was born. Almost as a miracle baby, he came to brighten the old age of his parents. It is not hard to imagine the love they had for him, and of course all those older brothers and sisters were as fond of the baby as people can be.

One evening after supper Mr. and Mrs. Robinson sat in their chairs on the front porch to enjoy the evening air. Little Billy Bob was about two at the time, a husky little boy with soft blond hair and merry blue eyes.

The child was playing about their feet, but in a moment of time he disappeared. They would miss him shortly . . . but it would be too late.

Suddenly, from the street side of the hotel they heard the scream of brakes and the sound of a car jerking to a stop. At the same time they heard a dull thud and they knew the car had hit something. They leapt to their feet and ran around the corner of the building.

To their horror they saw the driver of the car already out and holding a limp body in his arms. The stricken parents ran to his side to take the child, but the angels had already been there.

Two days later I stood with two or three hundred people in a sun-blistered little Texas cemetery. We had come to bury little Billy Bob. Somehow the pastor spoke his words, pronounced the benediction, and moved over to shake hands with the broken family.

Then it was that I heard the sermon. Mr. Sam stood up and lifted his face toward heaven. That tanned face was wet all over with tears as he looked up into the sky.

Then out of those tears I saw a smile. Mr. Sam was talking to God: "Thank You, Jesus," he said, "for letting us keep him as long as You did!"[5]

There was no recrimination, no bitterness, simply a reaffirmation of His relationship with God, in spite of the circumstances and sorrow of tragedy.

Where else is there to turn than to God in our need if we have also learned to turn to Him in our joys. If you have developed and nurtured a relationship with God during the good times you will discover that He is also there in the bad times.

Two Scottish Wigtown women, Mary Wilson and Agnes McLaughlin were martyred because of their faith, in the rising Solway ocean tide. Why? Because they refused to retract their Christian declarations.

The older woman was fastened to a stake much farther out than the younger, with the thought that when the younger saw the suffering and death struggle of her friend, she would recant.

Quickly the tide began to rise . . . to the older woman's waist, to her neck, to her lips, and then over her. The executioners called to the younger girl, "Look! What seest thou?"

Turning her head a little, she saw the struggles of her drowning friend and then gave her calm answer, "What do I see? I see the Lord Jesus Christ suffering in one of His members!" And she went to her death!

TODAY'S QUOTE: "God, give me hills to climb, and strength for climbing!" (Arthur Guiterman)

TODAY'S BIBLE VERSE: "When you pass through the waters, I will be with you; and when you pass through the rivers, they will

not sweep over you. When you walk through the fire, you will not
be burned; the flames will not set you ablaze. For I am the Lord your
God" (Isa. 43:2–3).

SUGGESTED BIBLE READING: Isaiah 43:1–28

13

How Ignorant Joshua Was

Little did Joshua know! Little did he know that morning what the events of this day would bring. It was not an unusual morning . . . like any other Mideastern sky, clean, clear, crisp.

The "Promised Land" was not large, actually it's merely a strip of semi-arid land separating the Mediterranean Sea from the vast sand wastes.

Joshua was not, by modern standards, a very intelligent man. He was definitely a primitive man, in a primitive culture, with primitive misconceptions. He knew very little about the planet on which he lived, its chemical compounds or its shape. He probably knew even less about the solar system. As far as he was concerned and most everybody in that day, the earth was flat. And for some inexplicable reason a little ball of fire called the sun rose on the eastern horizon and sank into the west some hours later. The sun rising, instead of the earth rotating, Joshua! What a silly misconception.

Little did Joshua know that the earth upon which he stood was a round sphere, 7,726 miles in diameter. He had no idea that there were close to 200 million square miles of surface area, with about 70 percent of that being water. He was unaware that those Canaanite hills were spinning on the axis of this earth in a cycle which took 23 hours, 56 minutes, and 4.09 seconds to complete. Little did he know that the whole mass of earth was then traveling through space as it was spinning at the rate of 18.5 miles per second!

Little did Joshua know that the sun which warmed his body was not a small traveling sphere, but a huge exploding ball of fire, 93 million miles away from the earth. He could not have conceived that at the core of the sun the temperature was over 30 million degrees Fahrenheit or that its diameter was 864,000 miles or that its volume was over 1,300,000 times that of this earth. Nor did he know that every 365 days, 6 hours, 9 minutes, and 9.54 seconds the earth makes one complete orbit around the sun.

BUT JOSHUA KNEW A NUMBER OF THINGS. . . . He knew that on this day God had promised him a victory over the powerful Amorite army.

As the battle raged on, Joshua and his army could see victory almost in their grasp, but they were running out of time. If they didn't defeat them before dark, the Amorites would have a chance to regroup and mount a new attack on the morrow. Joshua lamented as lots of people have, "If only we had more hours in the day!"

THEN . . . JOSHUA REMEMBERED WHAT HE DID KNOW. . . . He remembered His God! His God's power! His God's promises!

In front of all the people of Israel, Joshua, in a bold venture of faith that no one had ever attempted before, cried out to that brilliant, swirling ball of exploding hydrogen, "O sun, stand still over Gibeon, O moon, over the Valley of Aijalon" (Josh. 10:12)!

But Joshua, the sun remains constant . . . it's the earth that moves around the sun. Why didn't you say, "Earth, quit rotating on your axis?"

I don't know how it happened, nor can I explain what God did to make it happen . . . but it did!

You know, one of our major problems in our hurt, in our need, is that we know too much. We know how it can't happen, why it can't happen, scientifically how it is impossible, so we are even afraid to venture out in faith! Maybe we know too much about everything in our world and too little about God! We should trade some of our head knowledge with Joshua for some of his heart knowledge! And there has never been a day like this when God responded to His man!

How little Joshua knew. . . .

HE JUST KNEW HIS GOD! HIS GOD'S POWER! HIS GOD'S PROMISES!

TODAY'S QUOTE: "It is cynicism and fear that freezes life; it is faith that thaws it out, releases it, sets it free." (Harry Emerson Fosdick)

TODAY'S BIBLE VERSE: "The sun stopped in the middle of the sky and delayed going down about a full day. There has never been a day like it before or since, a day when the Lord listened to a man. Surely the Lord was fighting for Israel" (Josh. 10:13–14).

SUGGESTED BIBLE READING: Joshua 10:1–43

14

Love 101

On the first day of class, a college professor asked his "Speech 101" students to each introduce themselves and tell what they liked most and least about themselves. Each student, in turn, stood and did as requested. Finally the class attention focused on the next person, a young woman named Dorothy. She did not stand but kept her eyes glued to her desk. She did not look up. She did not say a word.

The professor thought perhaps she had not heard or perhaps she was a little shy and needed a bit of encouragement, "Dorothy, Dorothy, it's your turn." She did not respond. Then he said, "Come on Dorothy. How about you?"

After a long pause, she stood but did not turn to face the class. She said, "My name is Dorothy Jackson." Then she spun in the direction of the class, and with a sweeping hand she pulled her long hair away from her face. There for all to see was a large wine-colored birthmark covering nearly the entire left side of her face. She blurted out, "Now you all know what I like least about myself."

This sensitive, caring, professor moved to her side. He leaned over her shoulder and gave her a kiss on the birthmark and then gave her a big hug. He said, "That's okay. God and I think you're beautiful."

She began to cry, and she continued for many minutes. Other members of the class gathered around her and took turns giving her hugs. After she had gained her composure, she said, "Thank you. I have waited all my life for someone to hug me and say what you said. Why couldn't my parents have done that? My mother has never even touched my face."[6]

When Jesus Christ came in human form, He embraced us, kissed our ugly spots, and showed us the encompassing love of the Heavenly Father. "How great is the love the Father has lavished on us, that we should be called children of God" (1 John 3:1).

Whenever Jesus touched someone . . . something wonderful happened in that person's life. There are at least six different accounts or incidents when Jesus touched somebody else as recorded in the New Testament. Each is significant. Think of the impact His touch would have had on a leper.

Leprosy isn't very much a part of our world. But in Christ's day, being a "leper" had fearsome consequences. Lepers suffered from a disease which could take a finger, toes, hands, ears, even parts of the face. It often left its victims with a grotesque look. We have discovered it's because the nerves that register pain in the body have become damaged, so if a person with leprosy put a hand on a hot stove, there would be no pain, but considerable damage to the hand. It would literally be destroyed because there was no pain awareness. Lepers were outcasts, required to stay at a distance from healthy people. Whenever the leper noticed anybody coming near them, they were to cry out, "Unclean, unclean." They were rejected from society and family. No one ever touched a leper!

But Jesus did! And healing took place! Can you imagine what the literal human touch from Jesus must have done to his spirit, let alone to his body? I don't think Jesus simply reached out a finger to touch him with a tip . . . I believe Jesus reached for him and embraced him with a healing touch!

TODAY'S QUOTE: "Love sought is good, but given unsought is better." (William Shakespeare)

TODAY'S BIBLE VERSE: A man with leprosy came to Him and begged Him on his knees, "If you are willing, you can make me clean." Filled with compassion, Jesus reached out his hand and touched the man. "I am willing," He said. "Be clean!" (Mark 1:41–42)

SUGGESTED BIBLE READING: Matthew 20:1–34

15
Labels

Several management types were at the River Jordan as the crowds of people were coming out to hear John the Baptist, and they decided to get things organized.

So they set up tables and begin to give tags to those coming for repentance.

On the tag is to be written the person's name and #1 chief sin.

Bob walks up to the table. The organizers write his name on the tag and then ask, "What's your most awful sin, Bob?"

"I stole some money from my boss."

The person at the table takes a marker and writes in bold letters "EMBEZZLER" and slaps it on Bob's chest.

The next person steps forward. "Name?"

"Mary."

"Mary, what's your most awful sin?"

"I gossiped about some people. It wasn't very much, but I didn't like those people."

The organizers write, "Mary." Then, underneath the name, in large letters so that all the world can see, "GOSSIPER."

Another man steps up to the table. "Name?"

"George."

"George, what's your most awful sin?"

"I've really been thinking about how nice it would to have my neighbor's Corvette."

The tag is written, then slapped on his chest: "George . . . COVETER."

One more man shuffles up to the table. "What's your name?" he is asked.

"Gordon."

"Gordon, what's your number one sin?"

"I've had an affair with my secretary."

The organizer looks down, writes on his name tag, "Gordon . . . ADULTERER" and reaches over and slaps the sticker on his chest.

A woman, pitiful, stumbles up to the table. "Name?"

"Elizabeth."

"Liz . . . what's your most awful sin?"

"I've been dropping out."

The organizer writes: "Elizabeth . . . DRUGGIE."

"Next . . . hurry on, now."

The next man steps up to the table, "Your name?"

"John."

"What's your problem, John?"

"I've been beating my wife and kids."

This organizer scribbles, "John . . . ABUSER."

Soon, Jesus Christ, comes to be baptized. He walks down the line of those waiting to repent and be baptized and asks them for their sin tags. One by one, He takes those tags off the people and sticks them on His own body. He goes to John, and as He is baptized, the river washes away the ink from each name tag He bears.

TODAY'S QUOTE: "Salvation is free for you because someone else paid the price to set you free."

TODAY'S BIBLE VERSE: The next day John saw Jesus coming toward him and said, "Look, the Lamb of God, who takes away the sin of the world!" (John 1:29)

SUGGESTED BIBLE READING: Matthew 3:1–17

16

The Touch of the Master's Hand

It was battered and scarred, and the auctioneer
Thought it scarcely worth the while,
To waste much time on the old violin,
But he held it up with a smile.

"What am I bid for this old violin?
Who will start the bidding for me?
A dollar, a dollar, who'll make it two?
Two dollars, and who'll make it three?

"Three dollars once, three dollars twice,
Going for three," but no;
From the back of the room a gray-haired man
Came forward and took up the bow.

Then wiping the dust from the old violin,
And tightening up all the strings,
He played a melody pure and sweet,
As sweet as the angels sing.

The music ceased and the auctioneer
With a voice that was quiet and low
Said, "What am I bid for the old violin?"
And he held it up with the bow.

"A thousand dollars, and who'll make it two?
Two thousand, and who'll make it three?
Three thousand once, three thousand twice,
Going, and gone," said he.

The people cheered, but some of them said,
"We do not quite understand,
What changed its worth?" Came the reply,
"The touch of the master's hand."

And many a man with his life out of tune,
And battered and scarred with sin,
Is auctioned cheap to a thoughtless crowd,
Much like the old violin.

A mess of pottage, a glass of wine,
A game, and he shuffles along;
He's going once, and he's going twice,
He's going and almost gone.

But the Master comes, and the thoughtless crowd
Never can quite understand
The worth of the soul, and the change that is wrought
By the TOUCH OF THE MASTER'S HAND!
— Myra Brooks Welch

TODAY'S QUOTE: "We are saved by someone doing for us what we cannot do for ourselves." (Donald Lester)

TODAY'S BIBLE VERSE: "This is how God showed His love among us: He sent his one and only Son into the world that we might live through Him. This is love: not that we loved God, but that He loved us" (1 John 4:9–10).

SUGGESTED BIBLE READING: 1 John 4:1–21

17

Wet Pants Comfort

Come with me to a third grade classroom. There is a nine-year-old kid sitting at his desk, and all of a sudden there is a puddle between his feet, and the front of his pants are wet.

He thinks his heart is going to stop, because he cannot possibly imagine how this has happened. It's never happened before, and he knows that when the boys find out, he will never hear the end of it. When the girls find out, they'll never speak to him again as long as he lives.

The boy believes his heart is going to stop, so he puts his head down and prays this prayer: "Dear God, this is an emergency! I need help now! Five minutes from now I'm dead meat."

He looks up from his prayer and here comes the teacher with a look in her eyes that says that he has been discovered. As the teacher is coming to snatch him up, a classmate named Susie is carrying a goldfish bowl that is filled with water. Susie trips in front of the teacher and inexplicably dumps the bowl in the boy's lap. The boy pretends to be angry, but all the while is saying, "Thank You, Jesus! Thank You, Jesus!"

Now all of a sudden, instead of being the object of ridicule, this boy is the object of sympathy. The teacher rushes him downstairs and gives him gym shorts to put on while his pants dry out, and brings him back up to the room. All the children are on their hands and knees cleaning up around this child's desk . . . this sympathy is wonderful!

But as life would have it, the ridicule that should have been his has been transferred to someone else . . . Susie. She tries to help, but they tell her to get out. "You've done enough, you klutz!"

As the day progresses, the sympathy gets better and better and the ridicule gets worse and worse. Finally, at the end of the day, they are waiting for the bus and once again Susie has been shunned by the other children.

The boy walks over to Susie and whispers, "Susie, you did that on purpose, didn't you?"

Susie whispers back, "I wet my pants once, too."[7]

The Bible, as well as actual life experience, tells us that those who have been comforted are the very best kind of comforters to have around when comfort is needed. One of the best things about the fact that Jesus came to live among humans is that He identified with us, lived with us, discovered what it is to be human, and actually became a human being. What comfort that thought is to me when I need comfort. It's in how we look at it, it's all in perspective. Heaven understands what it is to hurt, to be embarrassed, to be humbled, to be rejected, to have nowhere else to turn when stressed.

All aspects of the person of Jesus Christ are so meaningful . . . but to me it is the ability to comfort us in our need which makes Him so attractive. I hope you have been able to sing the lines from this Gospel song:

> No one understands like Jesus. He's a friend beyond compare.*

How far away is His comfort and help? About as far away as a desperate nine year old's prayer!

TODAY'S QUOTE: "When you say a situation or a person is hopeless, you are slamming the door in the face of God." (Charles L. Allen)

TODAY'S BIBLE VERSE: "Praise be to the God and Father of our Lord Jesus Christ, the Father of compassion and the God of all comfort, who comforts us in all our troubles, so that we can comfort those in any trouble with the comfort we ourselves have received from God" (2 Cor. 1:4–5).

SUGGESTED BIBLE READING: 2 Corinthians 1:3–24

*Words/music by
John W. Peterson

18

The Face of God

After the horrible earthquake that devastated Ecuador in 1988, John Jackson, a photographer for the Indianapolis *Monday Morning* went there to cover the story. As he saw the human suffering he wrote a poem which was published in the October 10, 1988, issue.

> The line was long
> But moving briskly
> And in that line
> At the very end
> Stood a young girl
> About twelve years of age.
> She waited patiently
> As those at the front
> Of that long line
> Received a little rice
> Some canned goods
> Or a little fruit.
> Slowly but surely
> She was getting closer

To the front of that line,
Closer to the food.
From time to time
She would glance
Across the street.
She did not notice
The growing concern
On the faces of those
Distributing the food.
The food was running out.
Their anxiety began to show
But she did not notice.
Her attention seemed always
To focus on three figures
Under the trees
Across the street.
At long last
She stepped forward
To get her food
But the only thing left
Was the lonely banana
The workers were almost
Ashamed to tell her
That was all that was left

She did not seem to mind
To get that solitary banana
Quietly she took
The precious gift
And ran across the street
Where three small children
Waited
Perhaps her sisters
And a brother
Very deliberately
She peeled the banana
And very carefully
Divided the banana
Into three equal parts
Placing the precious food
In eager hands
Of those three younger ones
One for you
One for you
She then sat down
And licked the inside
Of that banana peel
In that moment I swear
I SAW THE FACE OF GOD!

TODAY'S QUOTE: "God is, and all is well." (John Greenleaf Whittier)

TODAY'S BIBLE VERSE: "And this is His command: to believe in the name of His Son Jesus Christ, and to love one another as He commanded us" (1 John 3:23).

SUGGESTED BIBLE READING: 1 John 3:1–24

19

Grace Enough for You

Paul the Apostle, one of God's choicest of servants, had to deal with a "thorn in the flesh." Was he alone? Not hardly. Life has a way of placing a thorn in every life. There was a cross even in the heart of God. The Saviour must wear a crown of thorns.

We soon discover that in this life there is no song without sadness; no garden without weeds; no rose without thorns; no days without pain; no person without strife; no eyes without tears; no happiness without grief; and no sky without clouds.

More thoughtful minds than mine have become convinced that pain is a necessary part in this whole plan of life. Suffering has made saints. Pain has matured character. Paul asked at least three times that his thorn in the flesh be removed. But beyond this asking, there is no record of Paul complaining or whining. He prayed! Affliction should drive us to our knees and to the Lord, not away from Him.

Oh, yes, there has been lots of speculation about the nature of Paul's "thorn." I've read that it was the fact that he was crippled, or a hunchback, possibly a midget, that he was blind, and one wag even put forth that it might have been his mother-in-law. We have no idea which is correct.

Well, was Paul's prayer answered? No and yes. Which? It was answered in a way that Paul didn't want, but spiritually in a way that has brought comfort and blessing to all kinds of people. "He said to me, 'My grace is sufficient for you, for my power is made perfect in weakness' " (2 Cor. 12:9)!

HE SAID TO ME. . . . This indicates the personal concern of Jesus Christ. In your hurt, how many times have you asked, "Does anybody really care? Does Jesus care?" The songwriter captured this concern like this:

> Does Jesus care when my heart is pained
> Too deeply for mirth or song?
> When for my deep grief I find no relief,
> Though my tears flow all the night long?

Then the chorus carries back the reply:

> Oh, yes, He cares, I know He cares.[8]

The Bible says that He is touched with the very "feelings" of our infirmities! What comfort!

MY GRACE IS SUFFICIENT FOR YOU. . . . Powerful, "My grace . . ." tells all of us for all time where the source of this grace comes from. Directly from the throne room of heaven. The same kind of grace exhibited in and through the life of Jesus Christ, "MY grace!"

The word "sufficient" is interesting. The supply has the exact correspondence with the need; never too much, never too little, never too soon, never too late; but timed to the tick of the clock and the beat of your human heart, it's sufficient! Grace for tomorrow's needs will not come today. Neither will grace for today arrive tomorrow!

"For you . . ." Not just for the present trial or test . . . but for you, yourself, personally, making you equal to the test. He doesn't alter trials, but He helps us to be equal to the test.

Don't pray for easy lives . . . pray to be stronger in person. Don't pray for easier tasks . . . pray for strength equal to the task. The working out of your life may not be something special, but you shall be a miracle.

Thorns, trials, tests, and temptations are all blessings, indeed, because they also bring the opportunity for the grace of Christ to perfect our character. God sends the grace along with the trial. Trials become triumphs! The very things that seem to break us are the things which really make us!

TODAY'S QUOTE: "As the earth can produce nothing unless it is fertilized by the sun, so we can do nothing without the grace of God." (Vianney)

TODAY'S BIBLE VERSE: He said to me, "My grace is sufficient for you, for my power is made perfect in weakness." Therefore I will boast all the more gladly about my weaknesses, so that Christ's power may rest on me (2 Cor. 12:9).

SUGGESTED BIBLE READING: 2 Cor. 12:1–21

20

How Grace Works

Some of the most comforting promises that God has made have been written about the promise of His presence with us in good times as well as bad times. For example, The Lord replied, "My Presence will go with you, and I will give you rest" (Exod. 33:14). There's lots more: "Your strength will equal your days. . . . The eternal God is your refuge, and underneath are the everlasting arms" (Deut. 33:25–27).

There is a story which comes to us from the second century, the martyr days of the church. It's about a condemned Christian who lay one night in his prison cell knowing that at daybreak he must be burned at the stake. The prospect was terrible. How could he endure the ordeal? He picked up the candle that flickered in his cell, and tried the experiment of holding his finger in the tiny flame. With a gasp of pain he quickly withdrew it. How could he possibly undergo the torture of his whole body given to the flames? Yet at sunrise he went to his death with irrepressible exuberance. From out of the circling flames, he testified to the all-sufficient grace of Christ and sang with a heavenly ecstasy shining from his face. When the real emergency came, sufficient grace was given to make him more than a conqueror. So it is always!

Divine grace is infinite and inexhaustible . . . but it is never dispensed superfluously. We must not expect the grace of God to be given for doing the needless.

Somebody once asked D. L. Moody, "Have you grace enough to be burned at the stake?"

Mr. Moody replied, "No."

The questioner pressed him further, "Do you wish you had it?"

"No," replied Moody again, "for I do not need it. What I need just now is grace to live in Milwaukee three days and hold a mission."

> My Lord has never said that He would give
> Another's grace without another's thorn:
> What matter, since for every day of mine
> Sufficient grace for me comes with the morn?
>
> And though the future brings some heavier cross,
> I need not cloud the present with my fears:
> I know the grace that is enough today
> Will be sufficient still through all the years.
>
> (Author is unknown)

Is the grace of God really sufficient in the most extreme of human experiences? A missionary writes:

On my arrival from China, I received a letter asking me

to call and see an invalid. I knew he was blind, but I was not prepared to see what I did see. He was lying upon the bed, every joint in his body immovable, unable to turn in any direction. But his mind was full of vigor, his heart full of grace of service. For 29 years he has been blind. Is it possible that such a one as he could do anything to help others? Listen: In India 17 children are supported by his efforts; 10 in China; a blind Bible-woman in Korea; a blind boy in the Sudan; a blind boy in Fiji; a blind Bible-woman in Jaffa. Three hundred pounds a year is received in answer to prayer by that faithful, sightless, silent, paralyzed disciple in that little shut-in room in Melbourne.

YES . . . God's grace is sufficient for YOU!

TODAY'S QUOTE: "There is nothing but God's grace. We walk upon it; we breathe it; we live and die by it; it makes the nails and axles of the universe." (Robert Louis Stevenson)

TODAY'S BIBLE VERSE: "May the grace of the Lord Jesus Christ, and the love of God, and the fellowship of the Holy Spirit be with you all" (2 Cor. 13:14).

SUGGESTED BIBLE READING: 2 Corinthians 13:1–14

21

Which Is the Greater Victory?

J. Sidlow Baxter, writer, speaker, pastor from Scotland, tells this story: Miss E. Wakefield MacGill of the Pocket Testament League was staying at my house, and told me the following remarkable story.

Years ago when her devout and gifted father was superintendent of a gospel mission in Glasgow, there was a great deal of trouble caused by a gang of young fellows in a slummy part of Glasgow, who were set on all kinds of mischief and violence. Even the police found it necessary to go in pairs or trios around the locality.

The gang of ruffians drank and gambled and fought and plotted and thieved and, among other things, was determined to smash up the revival which had broken out at the gospel mission under Mr. MacGill's faithful preaching.

The results, however, turned out the very opposite of what they anticipated. When some of them came as spies to the meetings, they fell under the power of the gospel and were either soundly converted to Christ or at least deeply convicted by the Holy Spirit.

In the end, every one of those godless young roughs and

criminals . . . a dozen or more in all . . . fell prey to Jesus and became saved.

This happened some 25 or 30 years before Miss MacGill's recent visit to my home in Edinburgh; and, gradually with the lapse of years, all those young terrorists, after being soundly saved, had become widely scattered from each other. But after all those years there comes to light at least one cheering and touching sequel, quite by coincidence.

Two men, seeing Miss MacGill's name advertised in connection with the recent meeting which she was to address in Edinburgh, found a flood of memories pouring into their minds at the sight of that name, "MacGill," and, all unknown to each other, decided to attend the meeting. These two men had both been members of that Glasgow gang years before and had never once seen each other in the meantime. The minute it was over they hastened to each other with unrestainable eagerness. With much emotion they shook each other by hand.

"Charlie!"

"Jim! Fancy, seeing you again after all these years!"

Then Charlie said, "Yes, praise the Lord, I'm still going on in the Christian life; and from the day of my conversion nearly 30 years ago until this minute I've never once had any further taste for the wretched drink!"

Jim's face clouded a bit at this, and a tear glistened in his eyes.

"Well, Charlie," he said, "I'm afraid I canna' say that. I only wish I could. There's never been one single day through all these years that I haven't had the thirst for drink." And then he quickly added, "But thank God, I'VE NEVER TOUCHED IT FROM THAT DAY TO THIS!"[9]

Now . . . which of these two men had experienced the bigger victory? Which of the two had the greater testimony to the grace and power of Jesus Christ?

God has different ways of dealing with our different temperaments and natures. He knows much better than we what is needed most by us. In one case He plucks up the evil propensity by the roots because He knows that this is the only way to set this prisoner free. In another case, he leaves the propensity there because the struggle and fight are necessary to develop a stronger Christian character.

God is the absolute emancipator . . . but He is also the infallible psychologist! He reads all of us like an open book. He knows what is the wisest path to take with each life.

Our responsibility to learn how to trust Him more fully so that time will prove His wisdom as well as His grace and power! There is always this promise that you will not be tempted above that which you are able to bear . . . but by His grace, His promise is that always, "My grace is sufficient for YOU" (2 Cor. 12:9).

TODAY'S QUOTE: "I need Thy presence every passing hour: What but Thy grace can foil the tempter's power?" (Henry Francis Lyte)

TODAY'S BIBLE VERSE: "And if by grace, then it is no longer by works; if it were, grace would no longer be grace" (Rom. 11:6).

SUGGESTED BIBLE READING: Romans 11:1–32

22

An Unorthodox Treatment

Norman Cousins became so sick that he was diagnosed as being "terminally ill" with about six months left to live. Every avenue of treatment had been exhausted in seeking for that one-in-500 chance for recovery.

He was aware that negative things such as fear, worry, depression, and anger could be a cause of disease and he wondered, *If illness can be caused by negativity, can wellness be created by positivity?*

He made the decision to begin taking control of his own treatment and so he devised a "laughter" therapy, because laughter was the most positive thing he knew about. Being in the media field, he had access to and watched all the funny movies he could get, read all the funny stories and books he could find, and asked all his friends to tell him something funny.

One thing he quickly discovered is that laughing for ten minutes released enough endorphins into his body that his pain was relieved for several hours. Following this regimen he recovered and lived for more than 20 years. If you would like to read how he did it, it's all in his book, *Anatomy of an Illness*.[10] Since this personal experiment and the book written to document it, other studies have confirmed what Cousins discovered: Laughter has a curative effect on the body, mind, soul, spirit, and emotions.

Norman Cousins simply re-discovered a truth that God has given to us long ago. "A cheerful heart is good medicine, but a crushed spirit dries up the bones" (Prov. 117:22). Some other translations flesh out this concept: "A rejoicing heart doeth good to the body" (YLT); "A joyful heart worketh an excellent cure" (RHM); and "A cheerful heart makes a quick recovery" (Knox). There you have it from the most reliable source in the universe . . . a cheerful, rejoicing, joyful heart is good for you and a great medicinal cure for your body! Try it . . . you may be surprised!

The word "rejoice" appears some 248 times in the Bible, the word "joy" about 200 times, the word "laugh" is penned some 40 times in the Bible.

To "laugh" is to: chuckle, giggle, roar, chortle, guffaw, snicker, titter, crackle, break up, roll in the aisle, howl, be joyful, merry making, mirth, belly laugh, and to split one's side.

Do you need strength — it's found in joy! Do you need help — it's found in rejoicing! Do you need to express the fruit of the Spirit in your life — do it joyfully! Do you need to celebrate — do it with happy people! Do you hurt — recovery is found in being joyful!

Dr. William Fry, psychiatrist at Stanford University Medical School, has given us a "laugh prescription." He says, "Laugh 100 times a day and you may feel like an idiot, but you'll be in great shape. In fact, you'll have given your heart the same workout you'd get if you pedaled on a stationary bike for 15 minutes. Over time, chuckling this much also lowers blood pressure and heart rate, reduces pain, strengthens the immune system, and cuts down on stress-creating hormones. Biggest problem: Finding that many things to laugh about," so says Dr. Fry.

To decide to laugh and treat yourself with laughter is an attitude, a mindset, a decision, and it will be a discipline! It's first an attitude . . . then an action! GO FOR IT!

TODAY'S QUOTE: "Laughter is a sacred sound to our God." (Tim Hansel)

TODAY'S BIBLE VERSE: "Though the fig tree does not bud and there are no grapes on the vines, though the olive crop fails and the field produce no food, though there are no sheep in the pen and no cattle in the stalls, yet I will rejoice in the Lord, I will be joyful in God my Savior" (Hab. 3:17–18).

SUGGESTED BIBLE READING: Habakkuk 3:1–19

23

Don't Quit!

When I read some parts of the Bible, such as Romans 8, an essence comes to mind that carries such concepts as: unconquerable, indomitable, insurmountable, invulnerable, unbeatable, undefeatable, invincible, and security. What does the writer of Romans mean? Simply that nothing can defeat you or destroy you when you are a child of God!

Many people are ready to give in or give up because of what they might be facing at the moment. There's a line from an old spiritual, "Nobody knows the trouble I've seen...." Yes, that might be true, there are lots of troubles, problems, and disasters in this world. And lots of people are beaten, defeated inside by life, and have no hope. Contrast that with others who, in spite of problems, never give up. If you get close to them, you will discover there are reasons for being undefeatable.

The will to live, which God placed in you when you were created, is one of the strongest of all human drives. But when you were born again, something further happened. God became one with you through the presence of His Son, Jesus Christ! Therefore one of the greatest qualities in the human being is the ability to persevere!

Fritz Kreisler was one of history's greatest violin virtuosos. As a young boy he wanted to play the violin, so his parents paid for his lessons for years. When he thought he was good enough, he tried out, but was refused many times for the lowliest position in a number of symphony orchestras. To earn money, he played in some cheap little dance orchestras.

Then, he decided to give up the violin and study medicine, at which he failed miserably. Next, he enlisted in the army and never was promoted higher than that of a private so when his enlistment was over, he quit. He tried his hand at some other things, which failed, too.

Still he wrestled with what he really wanted to do . . . play the violin. He finally went back to his former teacher and asked, "Will you teach me as though I know nothing?"

The teacher started with primary finger exercises, saying, "Fritz, if you truly want to be a great violinist, you must have the invincible, indefatigable idea that you will never quit!"

So he never did quit . . . until he was the man who graced such places as Carniege Hall in New York City.

"If God be for us, who can be against us?" One major secret to living and not giving up is to discipline yourself to integrate the Word of God into your spirit, listen: "The Spirit gives life; the flesh counts for nothing. The words I have spoken to you are spirit and they are life" (John 6:63). Your life can be changed by the living words of Jesus Christ! Hold them in your mind, hide them in your heart, meditate upon them, use them, repeat them, memorize them, live in them, think on them. Your life can be changed by the kinds of the living words you hold in your consciousness! And, finally . . .

DON'T QUIT

When things go wrong as they sometimes will;
When the road you're trudging seems all uphill;
When the funds are low, and the debts are high;
And you want to smile, but you have to sigh;
When care is pressing you, down a bit . . .
Rest if you must, but don't you quit!
Success is failure turned inside out;
The silver tint of the clouds of doubt;
And you never can tell how close you are;
It may be near when it seems afar.
So stick to the fight when you're hardest hit . . .
It's when things go wrong that you mustn't quit!

(Author is unknown)

TODAY'S QUOTE: "Nothing in the world can take the place of persistence. Talent will not; nothing is more common than unsuccessful men with talent. Genius will not; unrewarded genius is almost a proverb. Education will not; the world is full of educated derelicts. Persistence and determination alone are omnipotent!" (Calvin Coolidge)

TODAY'S BIBLE VERSE: "For everything that was written in the past was written to teach us, so that through endurance and the encouragement of the Scriptures we might have hope" (Rom. 15:4).

SUGGESTED BIBLE READING: Romans 8:18–39

24

His Name Shall Be Called Wonderful

"Wonderful" is a word that has been much overused in our day. Everything is tabbed as being wonderful. The word is almost threadbare . . . but it has never been used more adequately when it is used as a description of the Christ who was born, "And He will be called Wonderful Counselor, Mighty God, Everlasting Father, Prince of Peace" (Isa. 9:6).

If you or I could have arranged for the birth of Jesus to take place . . . it sure wouldn't have been in a stable. I would have chosen a nursery perfumed with Chanel No. 5, but God chose manure No. 6. Jesus was the King of all kings, yet there could not be found a room for Him in a boarding house. Jesus became what He was not, sin, so that we might become what we were not, saved.

During His life while here on earth, Jesus was the Bread of Life, yet He was hungry! He was the water of life, yet He went thirsty! He was the comforter, yet He wept! He could talk to the multitudes or to a single man up a tree or a woman beside a well. He wrote no books, but as you and I know, the presses of this world continue to grind out libraries about Him.

He made clay to anoint blind eyes . . . we took spit and blew it into His face. Men, like animals, pulled and plucked at His beard until blood ran down His cheeks. His hands touched fevered brows and blind eyes and paralyzed bodies . . . but human hands beat Him.

The Bible has almost 200 different names for the Son of God:

To the architect, Jesus is the "chief cornerstone."

To the artist, He is the "altogether lovely One."

To the baker, He is the "living Bread of Life."

To the banker, He is the "hidden treasure."

To the biologist, He is "the life."

To the builder, He is the "sure foundation."

To the doctor, He is the "great physician."

To the educator, He is the "great teacher."

To the engineer, He is the "new and living way."

To the farmer, He is the "sower and the Lord of the harvest."

To the florist, He is the "Rose of Sharon and the Lilly of the Valley."

To the sinner, He is the "Lamb of God who takes away the sins of the world."

And this is just the beginning! Do you need assurance . . . Jesus is here! Do you need healing . . . Jesus is here! Do you need encouragement . . . Jesus is here! Do you need to be lifted up . . . Jesus is here!

HIS NAME SHALL BE CALLED WONDERFUL . . .

They borrowed a bed to lay His head
When Christ the Lord came down,
They borrowed an ass in a mountain pass
For Him to ride to town,
But the cross that He bore
And the crown that He wore, were His own.
In the grassy mountain side,
He borrowed the dish of broken fish
With which He satisfied.
But the cross that He bore
And the crown that He wore, were His own.
He borrowed a room on the way to the tomb
The Passover lamb to eat,
They borrowed a cave for Him a grave
They borrowed a winding sheet,
But the cross that He wore
And the crown that He wore, were His own.
Yet though the cross that He bore and
The crown that He wore were His own,
THEY SHOULD HAVE BEEN MINE!

(Author is unknown)

TODAY'S QUOTE: "He changed sunset into sunrise." (Clement of Alexandria)

TODAY'S BIBLE VERSE: "For unto us a child is born. . . . And he will be called Wonderful Counselor, Mighty God, Everlasting Father, Prince of Peace" (Isa. 9:6).

SUGGESTED BIBLE READING: Isaiah 9:1–21

25

After the Tragedy Has Happened

Imagine . . . what is the worst tragedy that could happen to you? And this is not really the question: How can we, you and me, cope with the worst if it happens? When I'm looking for answers, I want to go to someone who is a practitioner, not a theorist, when it comes to offering some help or insight.

At age 32, William Cowper passed through a great crisis in his life. He attempted to commit suicide by taking the drug laudanum. Then he hired a horse-drawn cab, ordering the driver to take him to the River Thames where he would jump from the bridge . . . but they drove for about an hour in London's thick fog and were lost. In disgust, he got out to walk and found to his surprise he was almost at his own doorstep, they had gone in a circle.

The next morning, he took a knife and fell on the blade . . . but it broke and his life was spared again. Then he tried to hang himself and was cut down by a neighbor, unconscious but still alive. In his despair he finally turned to the Bible and at random opened it to read from Romans 10:10–13 and rejoiced in the forgiving power of Jesus Christ.

Some time later, Cowper summed up his faith in God's loving sovereignty in dealing with him by writing some of the great hymns of the church. Let me share some lines with you from one of his best:

> God moves in a mysterious way
> His wonders to perform;
> He plants His footsteps in the sea,
> And rides out the storm.
>
> You fearful saints, fresh courage take,
> The clouds you so much dread
> Are big with mercy, and shall break
> In blessings on your head.

There is still a time coming when God has promised to make all things new and beautiful. He knows that in time all pain, death, dying, sorrow, tears, tragedy, disease, adversity, storms, and tribulations will be removed! You, too, my friend, can endure the tragedies of the present by taking the promises of the God and envisioning a better tomorrow.

> JUST THINK . . .
> Of stepping on shore,
> And finding it heaven;
> Of taking hold of a hand,

And finding it God's hand;
Of breathing new air,
And finding it heavenly air;
Of feeling invigorated,
And finding it immortality;
Of passing from storm and
Tempest to an unbroken calm;
Of waking up . . .
And finding it HOME!

(Author is unknown)

TODAY'S QUOTE: "God's in His heaven . . . all's right with the world!" (Robert Browning)

TODAY'S BIBLE VERSE: "Do not let your hearts be troubled. Trust in God, trust also in Me. In my Father's house are many rooms; if it were not so, I would have told you. I am going there to prepare a place for you" (John 14:1–2).

SUGGESTED BIBLE READING: John 14:1–31

26

Don't Be Afraid

The person who knows no fear is not only a gross exaggeration . . . they might well be a biological impossibility! Here's a quote I found in a recent Kiwanis magazine: "Sometimes when I get in a nervous dither over such current problems as inflation, war, taxes, crime, pollution, political intrigue, urban sprawl, population, and whatever . . . I find myself yearning for 1933 when all we had to fear was fear itself."

Fear is a torment in the mind. It's a very real human emotion, fear stalks this land seeking out people who can be placed in bondage to fears. Fear is an enemy that we all need help in conquering, and for this we turn to God.

The Bible contains at least 365 places where it is written in one form or another, "Don't be afraid" or "fear not." That's one "don't be afraid" for every day of the year.

Tragedy had moved into a little family . . . the wife, mother had been taken by cancer, leaving the father and their four-year-old daughter alone. The funeral had taken place, family members had returned to their homes, it was evening, and for the first time, father and daughter were alone, just the two of them. It was bedtime and the little girl was not able to fall asleep in her room, alone. "Daddy

. . . can I come into your bedroom and sleep with you?"

He replied, "Honey, I don't know if that would be the best. How about if we moved your little bed into my bedroom for tonight?"

She agreed and they moved her bed and once more she settled down to sleep . . . but was too upset to sleep. She called out, in the darkness, "Daddy, are you still there?"

"Yes, honey, I am here."

Quiet for a long time, then, "Daddy, are you facing my direction?"

"Yes, honey," he replied.

She said, "That is good enough for me" and quickly fell asleep.

There is the tremendous cry from a hurting, human heart just to know that there is a presence nearby, particularly, a loving, caring, kind father. We, too, must know that in our hurt that God is there, too. We read it from the Word, "Don't be afraid; for I am with you!"

You must know that when fear comes flooding into your life . . . it doesn't come from God! Listen, "For God did not give us a spirit of fear (timidity), but a spirit of power, love, and self-discipline" (2 Tim. 1:7).

Fear is an unclean emotion which rips and tears at your peace of mind and well-being. Too much fear can also do physical damage to your inside. In contrast, look at what God provided to combat fears which stalk you: POWER, LOVE, and SELF-DISCIPLINE! The power is His power, the love is His love, and the self-discipline is our responsibility. If we will exercise the self-discipline here and not give way to fear, but in turn reject it in the power of God and apply the principles of His divine love, fear has to flee!

Pastor Bill Welsh relates this story: We have some friends who have a little boy who was born with a severe handicap that can cause him to go into a very violent seizure without any warning. The father would usually be the one holding their son during worship services and I remember on one particular occasion when the little guy started into a seizure, seeing the father get up with their son and with strong, yet gentle love, carry the boy to the back of the sanctuary where he held him close to his chest and rocked him, whispered to him and did all he could to help his son through the seizure.

One thing I noticed most of all was that there was not the beginning of a show of embarrassment or frustration in that father's face . . . only love for his hurting son, even though it caused a disturbance to others.

At that moment, I felt God speak to my heart in so many words something like this: "That's the way I love you through your imperfections. I'm not embarrassed to have people know that YOU are my son!"

TODAY'S QUOTE: "Love: Love is not blind . . . it sees more, not less. But because it sees more, it is willing to see less." (Rabbi Julius Gordon)

TODAY'S BIBLE VERSE: "And now these three remain: faith, hope, and love. But the greatest of these is love" (1 Cor. 13:13).

SUGGESTED BIBLE READING: 1 Corinthians 13:1–13

27

What About the Weeping?

Yes . . . it is true, even Christians can suffer loss, get hurt, experience tragedies, and die. Yes . . . even real, true believers grieve! Yes . . . people who have been born again weep.

You've no doubt heard it said that when a person comes to know Jesus as a personal Saviour that all tears are wiped away, that there will be no more losses, that we won't get hurt anymore, that we can have all the worldly goods we want. NOT! Not quite yet. We all are subject to such things that happen to others . . . and they happen to Christians, too. We all suffer losses. And when you do suffer your loss, whatever it may be, don't let anybody condemn you because your heart is aching or broken because of it. Don't be ashamed of your tears.

Your hurt may be recent . . . a child killed in an accident, a spouse taken by cancer, a son reduced to a vegetative state because of the drugs, a daughter who has run away, your own health which has been broken. Does Jesus sustain in such human experiences? YES! But life may still be shattered. The fact that we may be Christians doesn't make us immune from such feelings. Does God comfort when my heart is broken? YES!

Jesus is so very attractive to me . . . but the most appealing to me is His compassion. Our Lord never kicked anyone when they were down. He was a lifter! He said, "Come to me, all you who are weary and burdened, and I will give you rest" (Matt. 11:28). Thank You, Lord! All of us need His gracious invitation to find rest in Him . . . but never be ashamed of your tears!

> Ashamed of tears? This world of ours
> Might be as well ashamed of flowers;
> Skies of their stars when night appears,
> As mortals be ashamed of tears.
> For then, if ever, when we weep,
> We waken who have been asleep
> And let the flood of feeling roll
> Across the desert of the soul.
>
> We live so much the dull drab days,
> We walk so much life's treadmill ways.
> With heart so dumb, with mind so mute,
> We're little better than the brute.
> And then some day there comes some grief
> That only tears can give relief;
> And then the beauty floods our eyes
> That God has put in rain-washed skies.
>
> Anonymous

Ashamed of tears, when even He
Knelt weeping in Gethsemane?
We never see God quite so clear
As through the prism of a tear!
If purity we ever know,
It is our tears that made us so;
And only they need blush with shame
To whom emotion never came!

(Author is unknown)

TODAY'S QUOTE: "Great Spirit, help me never to judge another until I have walked two weeks in his moccasins." (Sioux Indian Prayer)

TODAY'S BIBLE VERSE: "Weeping may remain for a night, but rejoicing comes in the morning" (Ps. 30:5).

SUGGESTED BIBLE READING: Psalm 30:1–31:24

28

Take a Closer Look at the Oyster and the Pearl

Pearls are the product of pain! Pearls can be cultured or be found inside the shell of oyster on the ocean bottom somewhere. Whichever kind . . . it makes no difference. The pearl is produced the same way. If cultured, an alien substance is forced inside the shell and planted in the softness of the oyster. If collected from an ocean bottom, an irritant, perhaps a grain of sand, has slipped inside the shell. However, the process is the same. When it happens, the resources in the tiny sensitive oyster rush to that spot and begin to release healing fluids that would otherwise remain dormant. Soon, the irritant is completely covered and the wound has been healed and a pearl has been created!

No other gem or precious stone has such a fascinating history. Every pearl is the product of some irritant, some stress point, which at first hurt . . . then was healed. The pearl is a precious jewel conceived through hurt, irritation, born out of adversity, and nursed by an oyster that made adjustments. If there were no hurting . . . there could have been no pearl.

Some oysters have never been wounded, so what happens to

them? The people who fish and hunt for oysters simply discard them to become oyster stew or oysters-on-the-half shell for somebody's lunch.

An older couple was celebrating their 55th wedding anniversary and she was asked the secret of staying happily married for such a long time. She said, "Before we got married, there was a lot about John that irritated me, so I decided to write down a list of the ten most irritating things about John I didn't like, and decided that I would overlook these ten things. Well . . . I never got that list written out, so when he did anything that irritated me or made me angry, I would say, 'That's on this list, so I'll overlook that!' "

How are you handling the things in life that irritate? You know, if it weren't for the irritants in life we would all be very patient and kind and long-suffering, now, wouldn't we?

So . . . have you ever wondered why the entrance gates to heaven are made of pearls? Maybe such things don't interest you, but my mind tends to travel in such thoughts. But then, it's quite obvious that people who enter through those gates into Heaven will need no great theological explanations. They just know why!

The people who enter heaven's gates are the people who have been wounded, bruised, irritated, hurt, crushed, beaten . . . but have learned through the crucible of life how to respond to these strings of irritants. The adjustment phase has turned these problems into pearls. There these irritants have become pearls of testing and pearls of triumphant victory!

"The twelve gates were twelve pearls, each gate made of a single pearl" (Rev. 21:21). And come to think of it . . . there is no other way into Heaven except through one of these 12 gates of pearl. Those who have been through the fire, some through the flood, some through great sorrow, have all come through the blood of Jesus Christ to reach a heavenly home, not because of such problems but in spite of such deterrents. "He who overcomes will inherit all this, and I will be his God and he will be my son" (Rev. 21:7). What is to be overcome in order to be classified as a son or daughter? The obstacles that life has put in our path!

And the bottom line to be remembered is this: <u>PEARLS ARE THE PRODUCTS OF PAIN!</u>

TODAY'S QUOTE: "Troubles are often the tools by which God fashions us for better things." (Henry Ward Beecher)

TODAY'S BIBLE VERSE: "I saw the Holy City, the new Jerusalem, coming down out of heaven from God, prepared as a bride beautifully dressed for her husband" (Rev. 21:2).

SUGGESTED BIBLE READING: Revelation 21:1–27

29

The Story Did Not Die . . .

Charles Colson tells of a quiet act of forgiveness that began a chain that still survives. Deep inside one of Siberia's prison camps, a Jew by the name of Dr. Boris Kornfeld was imprisoned. As a medical doctor he worked in surgery and otherwise helped both the staff and the prisoners. He met a Christian, whose name is unknown, whose quiet faith and frequent recitation of the Lord's Prayer moved Dr. Kornfeld.

One day, while repairing a guard's artery which had been cut in a knifing, he seriously considered suturing it in such a way that he would bleed to death a little while later. Then . . . appalled by the hatred and violence he saw in his own heart, he found himself repeating the words of the nameless prisoner: "Forgive us our sins as we forgive those who sin against us."

Shortly after that prayer, Dr. Kornfeld began to refuse to go along with some of the standard practices of the prison camp, including turning in an orderly who had stolen food from a dying patient. After that he knew his life was in danger, so he began to spend as much time as possible in the relative safety of the hospital.

One afternoon he examined a patient who had just been operated on for cancer of the intestines, a man whose eyes and face reflected a depth of spiritual misery and emptiness that moved Kornfeld. So the doctor began to talk to the patient, telling him the entire story, an incredible confession of secret faith.

That night, someone sneaked in and smashed Dr. Kornfeld's head while he was asleep . . . he died a few hours later.

But Kornfeld's testimony did not die. For the patient who had heard his confession, became, as a result, a Christian. And he survived that prison camp and went on to tell the world what he had learned there. The patient was the great writer: Aleksandr Solzhenitsyn![11]

Forgiveness is one of the most powerful of human acts. And yet it can be outrageously costly. For forgiveness to be a real, true act extended to another, it cuts the offender off from the act and lets them go free. It is accepting the hurt, the loss, the pain inflicted by another, so that person can go free. But in an honest act of forgiveness . . . the surprise is that you, the offended are set free, too.

Sometimes for healing to take place, for restoration to begin, for a new beginning, there must be an act of forgiveness. This may be one of the most difficult things we can do because sometimes the only thing we have to hang on to is the thought of revenge or getting even with the person who did the hurting. This is the only act that I know of that can free a person from an unhappy, hurting past. This may be the only way to move unhindered into the future.

The decision to forgive is ours . . . the grace and strength to pull it off must come from God!

There's a story about Robert E. Lee, after the Civil War was over. He was visiting a Kentucky woman who took him to the remains of a grand old tree in front of her home. There she cried bitterly that its limbs and trunk had been destroyed by Federal artillery fire. She waited for Lee to condemn the North or at least sympathize with her loss. Lee paused, and then said, "Cut it down, my dear Madam, and forget it."

There are times when we need to let go of it and forget what is past so that we can face today and our tomorrows!

TODAY'S QUOTE: "We need to forget. . . . He who cannot forgive others breaks the bridge over which he must pass himself." (George Herbert)

TODAY'S BIBLE VERSE: "For if you forgive men when they sin against you, your heavenly Father will also forgive you" (Matt. 6:14).

SUGGESTED BIBLE READING: Matthew 6:1–34

30

The Blood of the Overcomer

Louis Pasteur's co-worker in the demonstration of what used to be called the "germ-theory" was Dr. Felix Ruh, a Jewish doctor in Paris. The physician's granddaughter died of black diphtheria, and Dr. Ruh, vowing that he would find out what killed his granddaughter, locked himself in his laboratory for days. He emerged with a fierce determination to prove, with his colleague Louis Pasteur, that the "germ theory" was more than a theory.

The medical association had disapproved of Pasteur and had succeeded in getting him exiled, but he did not go far from Paris. He hid in the forest and erected a laboratory in which to continue his forbidden research.

Twenty beautiful horses were led out into the forest of the improvised laboratory. Scientists, doctors, and nurses came to watch the experiment. Ruh opened a steel vault and took out a large pail filled with black diphtheria germs, which he had cultured carefully for months. There were enough germs in that pail to kill everybody in France. The scientist went to each beautiful horse and swabbed its nostrils, tongue, throat, and eyes with those deadly germs.

The scientists waited several days to see the outcome. Every horse developed a terrific fever, and all but one soon died. Most of the doctors and scientists wearied of the experiment and did not remain for what they thought would be the death of the last horse. The orderly on duty (while Ruh, Pasteur, and several others were sleeping on cots in the stables) had been instructed to awaken the scientist should there be any change in the animal's temperature.

About 2:00 a.m. the temperature showed a half-degree decrease, and the orderly awakened the scientists. By morning, the thermometer had dropped two more degrees, and by night the fever was gone entirely and the horse was able to stand, eat, and drink.

Then Dr. Ruh took a sledge hammer and struck that beautiful horse a death-blow between the eyes. The scientists drew all the blood from the veins of this animal that had developed the disease but had overcome it. The scientists were driven post haste to the Municipal Hospital in Paris. They bludgeoned their way past the superintendent and guards and forced entrance into a ward where 300 babies had been segregated to die from black diphtheria. With the blood of the horse they forcibly inoculated every one of the babies. ALL but three lived and recovered completely!

THEY WERE SAVED BY THE BLOOD OF THE OVER-COMER![12]

If there is to be any salvation, if there is to be any healing, if there is to be any eternal life for humans . . . it will be through the blood of the overcomer! Jesus Christ came to live among us so that

He could die for us. And in His death, by the shedding of His own blood . . . salvation was purchased for all who believe! And the Bible tells us that in that same sacrifice, we are healed! The prophet penned those immortal words, "By His stripes we are healed!" (Isa. 53:5).

So my hurting friend . . . if you have stayed with me to this point, lots of issues have been raised, lots of help and encouragement has been offered. But if you have not availed yourself of any of these offers or suggestions or biblical answers . . . it's not too late to do it now. There will be no help for your hurting unless we ultimately believe and put our hope and trust in the one-time sacrifice in which Jesus died for you! On an old rugged cross, He willingly laid down His life, willingly offered himself as the ultimate cure for sin and suffering of all humanity. You can appropriate that blood sacrifice . . . not by an inoculation, but by a spiritual experience, through an honest act of believing prayer. Do you believe He is the remedy for sin? Do you believe Him to be the healer of broken bodies and hurting hearts? THEN . . . through an act of faith, confess your need, invite Him to be your Saviour, the healer of your broken body and spirit.

Our last line, then is from 1 Peter 5:7, YOU, of the hurting heart, please "CAST ALL YOUR ANXIETY ON HIM BECAUSE HE CARES FOR YOU!"

TODAY'S QUOTE: "In His life, Christ is an example, showing us how to live; in His death, He is a sacrifice, satisfying for our sins; in His resurrection, a conqueror; in His ascension, a king; in His intercession, a high priest." (Martin Luther)

TODAY'S BIBLE VERSE: "For the message of the cross is foolishness to those who are perishing, but to us who are being saved it is the power of God" (1 Cor. 1:18).

SUGGESTED BIBLE READING: 1 Corinthians 1:4–31

Endnotes

[1] Charles Treptow, Angel Of Joy Lutheran Church, Lufkin, TX, *Parables, Etc.,* January 1996, p. 5.

[2] Ralph W. Harris, *Acts Today, Signs & Wonders of the Holy Spirit* (Springfield, MO: Gospel Publishing House, 1995).

[3] Alan Loy McGuinness, *The Friendship Factor* (Minneapolis, MN: Augsburg Fortress Publishers, 1979).

[4] Peter Marshall, *The Best of Peter Marshall* (Lincoln, VA: Chosen Books, 1983).

[5] John B. Wilder, *Stories for Pulpit and Platform* (Grand Rapids, MI: Zondervan, 1963).

[6] Gary T. Smalley and John Trent, *The Blessing* (Nashville, TN: Thomas Nelson Publishers, 1991).

[7] Dr. Robert Tuttle Jr., *Parables, Etc.*, 6/96, an actual account that happened in a Milwaukee school.

[8] Jay Lincoln Hall, "Does Jesus Care."

[9] J. Sidlow Baxter, *His Part and Ours* (London: Marshall, Morgan & Scott, Ltd., 1957).

[10] Norman Cousins, *Anatomy of an Illness* (New York, NY: W.W. Norton).

[11] Charles Colson, *Loving God* (Grand Rapids, MI: Zondervan, 1990).

[12] John Hendee, *Ambassadors for Christ: Peace Treaty With God* (Cincinnati, OH: Standard Publishing, 1984).